THE TRUE STORY OF AN AMAZING ALL-BROTHER BASEBALL TEAM

BROTHERS AT BAT

Written by **Audrey Vernick** ♦ Illustrated by **Steven Salerno**

Clarion Books • Houghton Mifflin Harcourt • Boston New York • 2012

Clarion Books

215 Park Avenue South. New York, New York 10003

Text copyright © 2012 by Audrey Vernick
Illustrations copyright © 2012 by Steven Salerno

Clarion Books is an imprint of Houghton Mifflin Harcourt Publishing Company.

www.hmhbooks.com

The text of this book is set in Bernhard Modern.
The original illustrations for this book were created with black crayon, gouache, watercolor, and pastel
on Arches 260 lb. hot press paper, with added digital color rendered in Adobe Photoshop CS-4.

Library of Congress Cataloging-in-Publication Data
Vernick, Audrey.
Brothers at bat : the true story of an amazing all-brother baseball team / by Audrey Vernick ; Illustrated by Steven Salerno.
p. cm.
ISBN 978-0-547-38557-0
1. Acerras (Baseball team) 2. Baseball teams—United States—History. 3. Brothers—United States—Biography—Juvenile literature.
4. Baseball teams—New Jersey—History. 5. Brothers—New Jersey—Biography—Juvenile literature. I. Salerno, Steven, ill. II. Title.
GV875.A43V37 2012
796.35709749—dc23
2011025645

Manufactured in Singapore
TWP 10 9 8 7 6 5 4 3 2 1
4500326174

For the Acerras of the past, present, and future —A.V.

To my father, Joseph Paul Salerno (Pop),
the athlete of the family —S.S.

WHEN WINTER'S CHILL melts into spring, back doors swing
open and slap shut as kids just home from school run outside—
mitts, bats, and balls in hand.

In one New Jersey town near the ocean, back in the 1920s and '30s, you could hear the same door slam over and over. Three brothers raced out.

Out went three more.

And more:

And still more.

It sounds like a fairy tale: twelve baseball-playing brothers. But Anthony, Joe, Paul, Alfred, Charlie, Jimmy, Bobby, Billy, Freddie, Eddie, Bubbie, and Louie Acerra were real.

They had four sisters, too: Catherine, Florence, Rosina, and Frances. And a white dog . . . named Pitch! The sisters didn't play ball. Back then, most people thought sports were just for boys.

The Acerras had so many kids that they slept two to a bed
and sat three across in their outdoor bathroom. They ate dinner
wherever they could find a seat. Even on a baseball field, there were
more boys than positions.

But that didn't stop them from playing.

Baseball set the rhythm of their lives.

"Every spring," Freddie said, "you would take your glove out, go in the yard, and play." Neighbors couldn't recall a time when there weren't Acerra boys outside tossing the ball, hitting it hard, racing around—with the young ones watching, wishing they were old enough to play.

Their high school baseball team had an Acerra on it twenty-two years in a row!

Anthony AGE 32

Joe AGE 27

Paul AGE 24

Alfred AGE 22

Charlie AGE 20

Jimmy AGE 18

Bobby AGE 16

Billy AGE 15

Freddie AGE 13

Eddie AGE 12

Bubbie AGE 10

Louie AGE 7

In 1938, the brothers ranged in age from seven to thirty-two. The oldest nine formed their own semi-pro team and competed against other New Jersey teams. Their father coached them and never missed a game.

Their uniforms all
said the same thing: Acerras.

The infields they played on were dirt; outfields were littered with rocks and sand. The brothers loved to talk about the day they played at "the old dog track," an oceanfront stadium that had once been an auto raceway. It was there that Anthony, the oldest, hit a couple of home runs right into the Atlantic Ocean.

They called Anthony "Poser" because of the way he'd stand at the plate—as if his baseball-card photo were being taken.

Charlie, the fifth oldest, was the slowest brother. He was a good player, but a terrible runner. The brothers often joked about the time he hit a ball nearly out of the park, but only made it to second.

Jimmy, the sixth brother, had a knuckleball people *still* talk about. "You couldn't hit it," Eddie said. "You couldn't catch it, either." That ball danced in the air. Jimmy was a great hitter, too, probably the best player on the team.

But there was no jealousy, no rivalry, no fighting. As the younger brothers grew up, the older ones shared playing time. If someone dropped a fly ball or struck out, no one screamed or threw down his glove or stomped off the field. "We stuck together," Freddie said.

The team played around New Jersey, in New York, Connecticut, wherever they could find a good game. Paul sent out letters, looking for new teams to play. The all-brother team always drew big crowds.

In 1939, at the New York World's Fair, the Acerras were honored as the biggest family in New Jersey. They were taken to the Newark airport, where they boarded a plane and were flown over the fairgrounds. They couldn't believe it—no one they knew had been on a plane before! Most of the people at the World's Fair, looking up at that small plane in the sky, had no idea there was a whole team of brothers aboard.

But it wasn't all fun and games and sunny skies. Their darkest day occurred on the field, too.

Freddie was on third base in a scoreless game. Alfred was at the plate. He touched his shoulder—the signal that he was going to bunt.

Then things went wrong.

The pitch came in high, and somehow the ball bounced off the bat and hit Alfred hard, right in the face.

They rushed him to the doctor, but he lost an eye. For the next few months, Eddie took Alfred's place as catcher. Everyone thought Alfred's baseball days were over.

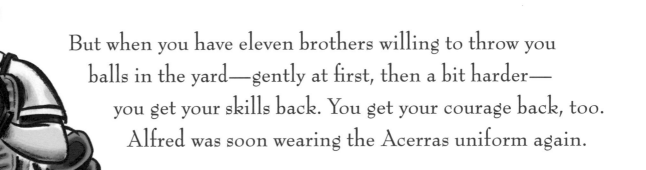

But when you have eleven brothers willing to throw you balls in the yard—gently at first, then a bit harder— you get your skills back. You get your courage back, too. Alfred was soon wearing the Acerras uniform again.

"He was a pretty good catcher for a guy with one eye," Freddie said.

In the 1940s, something pulled the brothers' attention away from baseball. American soldiers were fighting in the Second World War across the Atlantic— that same huge ocean Poser had hit baseballs into.

Battles were raging and soldiers were dying, but the brothers knew it was important to fight for their country.

The team disbanded as six Acerra brothers joined the service. Poser was the first to go. He, Charlie, Eddie, and Bobby all served in the Army. After Billy joined the Marines, Freddie did, too.

EUROPE

ATLANTIC

Those six brothers traveled far from home. After a lifetime of talking and playing together every day, they now went months—years!—without seeing one another. They longed for the salty-stew smell of the Atlantic Ocean.

They dreamed of their childhood home, of the back door *slap slap slapping* as they ran outside to play. And of long afternoons, throwing a ball in high, soaring arcs from glove to glove to glove in a field full of brothers.

Back in New Jersey, their parents and siblings waited for news. It took a long time for letters to reach them from overseas. There was a lot of time to worry.

When the war finally ended, everyone was so happy. Eddie, out in California with the Army, was so excited that he went up to women he didn't even know and kissed them!

Many American soldiers died in World War II, but the Acerras were very lucky.
One by one, all six brothers returned from their time in the service.
Mama Acerra cried each time a boy walked in the door.

By the summer of 1946, the family was ready to get back to baseball.
They were all older, of course, and Poser's heart had grown weak, so now he
coached the team.

They joined the Long Branch City Twilight Baseball League and over the next six years won the league championship four times.

Every Sunday, crowds filled the stands to watch the all-brother team play.

As time passed, the Acerras got married and moved into their own homes.
They worked hard at their jobs—at the water company, at the post office,
selling insurance. They started having children of their own.

In 1952, they played their last game as a team.
But they had already made history.

History?

It's true.

The Acerra brothers were the longest-playing all-brother baseball team ever.

In 1997, the Baseball Hall of Fame held a special ceremony to honor them. Only seven were still alive. Paul, Alfred, Bobby, Billy, Freddie, Eddie, and Bubbie all made the trip, along with more than a hundred relatives, including their sister Frances.

Jimmy's son donated his father's uniform and glove, which were put on display, right there in the same museum that honored Babe Ruth and Ty Cobb and Willie Mays. "They treated us like we were kings," Freddie said.

After such a thrilling day, you could picture them
driving off into the sunset, happily ever after.

But their bus broke down.

They could have sat on the curb, grumbling in the summer heat.

But someone found a bat and ball, and as three generations
of Acerras waited for a new bus, they played ball.

That ball soared from grandfather to granddaughter, from father to son.
From brother to brother.

AUTHOR'S NOTE

According to the National Baseball Hall of Fame, from the 1860s until the 1940s, there were twenty-nine baseball teams made up entirely of brothers. The Acerras played longer than any other.

They were fortunate to play at a time when there was great interest in hometown teams. Local games were a source of enormous community pride. The story of Long Branch, New Jersey, is seldom told without a mention of those Acerra boys.

I came across their story when my husband and Bobby Acerra's son Rob founded a much-needed recreational baseball league in our town. I learned about the brothers' amazing history and I wanted to tell their story.

I discovered that one brother, Freddie, lived nearby. Nervous about intruding on a stranger's life, I called to ask if I could interview him. Without hesitating, Freddie explained he had an open-door policy for dinner. He cooked for his brother Eddie, other family members, former coworkers, and any hungry friends three nights a week. He suggested I come on Tuesday, pasta night.

It was a night of spaghetti with Freddie and Eddie.

They recalled some very specific details with sharp accuracy. When talking about Alfred's time at bat on that disastrous day, Freddie remembered wondering, while standing on third, why his brother was bunting.

Listening to the brothers relive their glory days has been a deeply satisfying treat and a vitally important part of writing this book. Throughout the process, the good people in the research library at the Baseball Hall of Fame were also of enormous help, especially the director of research, Tim Wiles, with an awesome late-innings assist from Mary Bellew.

What the Acerra brothers achieved is remarkable. But when you meet them, what impresses you most is their strong sense of family. And pride.

Jimmy's daughter Pat said, "We were all raised to be team players, no matter what situation we were in—at work, at play, at war, in relationships—you carry that spirit with you. And it's part of you. That spirit was inspired in everyone who knew the Acerra brothers."

ARTIST'S NOTE

While creating the period illustrations for this book, I thought about my father, Joe, and his brothers, Paul and Pasquale (Pat), the Salerno boys of Kennedy Road in Port Henry, New York. In the 1940s they played for the Port Henry High School football, basketball, and baseball teams, and then for the Town Team (semi-pro) baseball and basketball teams. The three brothers served in the U.S. military during World War II and the Korean War, each returning home safely. Uncle Pat went on to play professional baseball for several Brooklyn Dodgers Minor League teams for six years in the 1950s, and Uncle Paul was offered a contract to pitch for a St. Louis Browns Minor League team. My father played football for a U.S. Army team. He also excelled in golf, winning twenty club championships at four different clubs over a span of five decades, and to date has scored five holes in one.

Front row (from left): Bubbie, Charlie, Alfred, Freddie, Louie **Back row:** Joe, Anthony, Jimmy, Billy, Paul **Standing:** Bobby (left), Eddie (right)